DALIT GIRLS' EDUCATION IN INDIA

BY

Theresa Ferry

Submitted to the

Faculty of the College of Arts and Sciences

of American University

in Partial Fulfillment of

the Requirements for the Degree of

Master of Arts

In

International Training and Education

Chair:
_____
Charles Tesconi

_____
Lynn Cohen

_____
Dean of the College of Arts and Sciences

_____
Date

2008

American University

Washington, D.C. 20016

UMI Number: 1455140

Copyright 2008 by
Ferry, Theresa

All rights reserved.

INFORMATION TO USERS

The quality of this reproduction is dependent upon the quality of the copy submitted. Broken or indistinct print, colored or poor quality illustrations and photographs, print bleed-through, substandard margins, and improper alignment can adversely affect reproduction.

In the unlikely event that the author did not send a complete manuscript and there are missing pages, these will be noted. Also, if unauthorized copyright material had to be removed, a note will indicate the deletion.

UMI Microform 1455140
Copyright 2008 by ProQuest LLC.
All rights reserved. This microform edition is protected against unauthorized copying under Title 17, United States Code.

ProQuest LLC
789 E. Eisenhower Parkway
PO Box 1346
Ann Arbor, MI 48106-1346

© COPYRIGHT

by

Theresa Ferry

2008

ALL RIGHTS RESERVED

DALIT GIRLS' EDUCATION IN INDIA

BY

Theresa Ferry

ABSTRACT

Dalits, formerly known as 'untouchables', are one of the most marginalized groups in Indian society. Dalit girls in particular have been viewed in Indian society as passive victims of caste and gender discrimination. Some Dalit groups, however, have considered Dalit girls as having agency to make choices in their lives. This study considers what Dalit girls have to say about discrimination against them as well as the role that education plays in overcoming that discrimination. This qualitative study involved observing and interviewing seven Dalit girls in a Gujarati vocational school (Dalit Shakti Kendra), interviewing Dalit leaders in India, and analyzing literature to understand interrelated factors among caste, economic status, and gender. The results of this study suggest that education can help Dalit girls to find more economic opportunities and overcome hardships in their lives, but the extent to which education can help them overcome caste and gender discrimination is questionable.

ACKNOWLEDGEMENTS

I would like to thank my committee members, Charlie Tesconi and Lynn Cohen for graciously contributing their time to support the writing of my thesis, and for their constructive feedback. I would also like to thank the members of my Pro-Seminar class for encouraging me to pursue this study. I extend my sincere gratitude to Robyn Mathias, who funded my thesis research in India. Finally, I thank the administrators at Dalit Shakti Kendra in Gujarat who allowed me to interview students at their school.

TABLE OF CONTENTS

ABSTRACT... ii

ACKNOWLEDGMENTS.. iii

LIST OF TABLES... v

CHAPTER

    1. INTRODUCTION AND CONTEXT... 1

    2. LITERATURE REVIEW... 10

    3. METHODOLOGY.. 40

    4. RESULTS AND DISCUSSION... 49

    5. CONCLUSIONS... 62

REFERENCES.. 70

LIST OF TABLES

TABLE

2.1 Health Statistics on Manual Scavenging...	23
2.2 Economic Deprivation of Dalit Women..	24
2.3 Basic Literacy Rate of Dalits (%)...	28
2.4 Literacy Trend from 1961-1991..	28
2.5 SC Enrollment in Higher Education 1995..	29
2.6 Government Education Policies..	32
3.1 Methodology...	40
3.2 DSK's Objectives and Programs...	42
3.3 Enrollment in DSK Vocational Courses as of 2007...........................	44
4.1 Forms of Discrimination against Dalit Girls Interviewed	59
4.2 Role of Education to Overcome Discrimination................................	61
5.1 Major Choices Made by Girls Interviewed..	65
5.2 Advocacy Strategies of Dalit Organizations......................................	67

CHAPTER 1

INTRODUCTION AND CONTEXT

With a population of over one billion, India has the second largest education system in the world. In the public education system there are over one million schools, 17,000 colleges and 329 universities in the country (Council for Social Development, 2006, p.34). The Indian Government is concerned with attending to the diverse needs of individuals within this massive system. India's National Policy of Education states, "Each individual's growth presents a different range of problems and requirements, at every stage from the womb to the tomb. The catalytic action of education in this complex and dynamic growth process needs to be planned meticulously and executed with great sensitivity" (Government of India, 1998, p.3). Despite these intentions, major social factors limit the Government's ability to address the multitude of educational needs of marginalized groups.

Huge inequalities exist in the education system, stemming from factors related to social background, income, gender, place of residence, and caste (Kapadia, 1995). Caste is a social institution, not a legal one, which is reproduced socially and culturally. Six major characteristics of the caste system include the following: segmental division of society, hierarchy, restrictions on feeding and social intercourse, civil and religious disabilities and privileges, lack of unrestricted choice of occupation, and restriction on marriage (Seenarine, 2004).

Dalits, formerly known as the untouchables, are considered the lowest social class in India. The term Dalit literally means "broken or reduced to pieces" (Seenarine, p.35). The caste system ascribes a "pure" status to those from higher castes and a "polluted" status to Dalits. The purity-pollution scale leads to a broad set of social sanctions among castes in India (Shah *et al*, 2006). The continuing discrimination against Dalits is one such factor. According to the Indian Census of 2001, Dalits make up 16% of the Indian population, yet their socio-economic and political status sets them apart from the upper castes.

Caste discrimination against Dalits is strongly pronounced. Exclusion, subordination, and exploitation are common (Shah *et al*, 2006). The practice of "untouchability", of physically separating those among the lowest and higher castes, was legally abolished in India over 50 years ago, yet Dalits continue to be treated as impure members of society (Subramanian, 2006, p.5).

Education exclusion is pronounced among Dalit girls. A 1994 survey on school participation among rural children showed that nearly 50% of Dalit girls (aged 5-14) dropped out of school, contrasted with 36% of other rural girls (Nambissan, 2003). Cited reasons for this disparity were mainly economic. Nambissan (2003) also holds that Dalit or Adivasi (tribal) status coupled with poverty compounds educational deprivation (p.118).

In 1937 the term 'Scheduled Castes' (SC) became a legal term to designate the list of lowest ranking Hindu castes who would be given special protection and support by the Indian Government (Chanana, K., 1993, p.122). In addition, the term

'Scheduled Tribes' (ST) was introduced in 1947 to recognize the "backward tribes" of India, meaning those tribes who are socially and economically deprived (*ibid*). Today, all educational institutions must reserve 15% of seats for SC and 7.5% for ST (Chanana, 1993). The preferential treatment of SC and ST is called the "policy of reservations". Chanana (1993) notes that a controversy in the policy of reservations is that women are not mentioned specifically, except under Article 15 of the Constitution (p.124).[1]

While there have been policy responses in the 1990s to address the needs of scheduled castes (SC) at all schooling levels, these policies have not been considered as enabling forces that address the social norms of discrimination among disadvantaged groups (Chopra & Jefferey, 2005, p.63). Government reservations for minority groups' access to education may help to increase the number of Dalit girls in school, but they do little to achieve the much needed inclusion of this marginalized group. Annamalai (2002) notes that these safeguards of the Indian constitution are ineffective because "the power structure of law-enforcement agencies and the prejudice of the general public make it almost impossible for Dalits to get legal redress from discrimination" (p.2). While some groups have viewed Dalits as passive victims of discrimination and oppression, others have focused on their active involvement in Indian society.

---

[1] Article 15 says, "The State shall not discriminate against any citizen on grounds only of religion, race, caste, sex, place of birth, or any of them" (Government of India, 1950).

Ideological Shift

There has been a shift in ideology around Dalit's status from being passive victims of discrimination to active advocates for their rights (Annamalai, 2002). Gandhi originally called the untouchables "harijan" meaning "people of God". This term carried a passive connotation in Indian society. The term Dalit, however, is seen as a political term that represents a shift in ideological thinking about Dalits (*ibid*). As Annamalai (2002) states, the Dalit Movement "emphasizes asserting a separate identity and inculcating pride in Dalit cultural traditions" (p.2). Educated Dalits use a variety of visible means to raise awareness about their situation, including conferences, book and journal publications, action groups, and websites (*ibid*).

Seenarine (2004) portrays women as active agents in making choices in their lives, rather than being viewed as passive victims of oppression. He interviewed rural Dalit women about their social and economic characteristics and views of education to better understand how they resist domination and negotiate access to education and economic resources (p.6). He writes, "both women and Dalits have been defined as impure, of sinful birth, and as having a polluting presence" (p.39). He holds that the educational and employment gains that Dalit women have made since independence are due to female resistance to oppressive forces (p.42). This study provides evidence that poor Dalit women are making strides toward greater autonomy in Indian society.

Perhaps the most compelling example of giving Dalit girls agency to make their own life decisions comes from Dalit Shakti Kendra, a vocational school in the state of Gujarat. Martin Macwan, a Dalit activist, started the school as a way to help Dalit youth to better understand their identity. The school initially was aimed to help those Dalits who were manual scavengers, or the lowest class citizens who are relegated to the degrading work of cleaning up human and animal excrement. Most manual scavengers are women. Dalit Shakit Kendra provides Dalit girls with the opportunity to learn skills which will help them find economic alternatives to manual scavenging (Manecksha, 2006). Macwan also encourages Dalit youth to gain social literacy on Dalit empowerment while building their vocational skills.

Statement of the Problem

Caste, economic status, and gender discrimination may exclude Dalit girls from educational opportunities. As a marginalized group, Dalit girls have first-hand experience of how this discrimination makes them vulnerable in Indian society.

What needs to be documented more clearly is how discrimination against Dalit girls affects their educational opportunities. By documenting their stories of discrimination, we will be better able to understand how and if education helps girls overcome oppression. Rather than looking at Dalit girls' education with a deficit lens of what is not in place or what needs to be fixed, this study considers what is being done in schools to help Dalit girls overcome discrimination.

Purpose of the Project

This study seeks to address the following questions:

1. How do caste, economic status, and gender interrelate?
2. What do Dalit girls have to say about discrimination against them?
3. To what extent do Dalit girls see education as helping them to overcome discrimination?

There have been increased advocacy efforts to raise awareness of the social exclusion faced by Dalits in general over the last fifteen years. Some address the problem of social exclusion as stemming from a lack of curriculum on Dalit life histories, language, and culture. Other efforts challenge caste ideology and its dominance in Indian school systems.

This study attempts to better understand Dalit girls' educational experiences from their own perspective. The purpose of the first question is to understand interrelated factors between caste, economic status, and gender. The second question considers what stories of discrimination tell us about Dalit social reality. The third question seeks to document how educational opportunities may or may not help Dalit girls to overcome discrimination. This study considers Dalit girls' perspectives in order to show that their voice has value in Dalit education studies and Dalit advocacy initiatives.

Significance of the Study

Girls' education in its own right is important to address because it can enhance human and economic development, and it has been shown to lower fertility and mortality rates (Chopra & Jeffery, 2005, p.19). This is not meant to imply that boys' education is not important; Dalit girls and boys share many challenges in terms of educational opportunities. Focusing specifically on Dalit girls, however, will hopefully bring greater gender awareness to Dalit education studies.

The study is particularly useful for NGOs, grassroots activists, and policymakers who are working with Dalit girls and women throughout India. Of particular significance are the Dalit Foundation, Dalit Freedom Network, All India Council of Churches, and Navsarjan, who have shown interest in this study.

Freire's Education Model

This thesis draws on Paulo Freire's philosophy of raising the consciousness of individuals to understand their own place in society and recognize their oppression. Freire (1997) writes, "Problem-posing education, as a humanist and liberating praxis, posits as fundamental that the people subjected to domination must fight for their emancipation" (p.67). Human beings should not be objects of history but subjects of their own reality (p.66). Freire's education model emphasizes dialogue as a key to conceptualization and action.

Limitations

There are a few limitations to this research paper. First, girls interviewed in New Delhi and Gujarat represent a very small population within the Indian subcontinent. If this was a sustained project that spanned the course of more than one year, interviews would be conducted in geographically diverse regions of the country in order to make more informed generalizations about Dalit girls' education and advocacy.

A second limitation is that the researcher is a Western woman with a working knowledge of Dalit studies. She has had one year's experience teaching in Mussoorie, India, a hill station in the north of the country, but in general she has had limited interaction with the Dalit population. Third, the language barrier is a limitation in this study. The researcher does not speak Gujarati, the language spoken by most of the Dalit girls who were interviewed. A translator interpreted the interviews. Finally, data on Dalit education is somewhat outdated. Available data is mainly from the early 1990s. More recent data would portray more accurately the educational status of Dalit girls today.

Definitions

Key definitions used in this paper are listed below.

caste	A birth-ascribed system of socially stratifying groups based on the Varna system of Hindu ideology
Dalit	The lowest social group in India, formerly called the untouchables.

equity	Fairness of educational opportunities and systems.
gender	Gender is defined both as a biological, ascribed status, as well as a social concept that "is created and recreated in the interactions between women and men that determine gender relations" (World Bank, 2005).
ideology	An interrelated set of ideas, beliefs, and values typically interwoven with claims or theses and presented as an explanation for something; sometimes ideology reflects the socio-political needs and aspirations of an individual, group, class, or culture (Tesconi, 2007).
Jati	A sub-caste or closed social group into which one is born and within which one must marry (Kinsley, 1993, p.188).
Sati	Burning of widow with her deceased husband.
social exclusion	Social exclusion refers to how exclusion from social relationships can "exacerbate people's experiences of inequality, poverty, and capability deprivation" (Chopra & Jeffrey, 2005, p.62).
stratification	The structuring of society on the basis of differential social status of various groups (Srirama, 2007, p.48).
Varna	Indian term for the four main castes: Brahmin, Kshatriya, Vaishya, and Shudra

CHAPTER 2

LITERATURE REVIEW

This chapter reviews literature on Dalit girls' education in India, which will be covered in three parts. In the first part of the literature review, an overview of caste and untouchability is presented. Second, economic status and gender are explored, followed by an analysis of the interrelated factors among caste, economic status, and gender. Third, strategies to promote the education of Dalit girls will be reviewed, including government policies and advocacy initiatives.

Part I: Caste and 'Untouchability

The most salient themes about caste that emerge from the literature deal with its history, hierarchical nature, and how religious, economic, and political life are influenced by caste. These main issues will be explored in this section.

Caste as a Social System

The caste system in India has existed for over 2,000 years. Based on the Varna system of Hinduism, India's caste sytem includes the following four divisions: Brahmans (the priestly caste), Kshatriyas (the warrior caste), Vaishyas (the trading caste), and Shudras (the servile caste). In addition to this division, the post-independent government identified nearly 3,400 castes and sub-castes in India.

Among the 160 million Dalits in India there are over 1,000 castes and sub-castes (Seenarine, 2004).

According to Berreman (1979), Hinduism justifies the caste system. The concepts of dharma and karma and purity and pollution demonstrate this. Dharma refers to "one's religious/moral duty to fulfill to the best of one's ability the obligation inherent in the status to which one has been born – especially caste and sex status"; karma refers to reaping what one sews or "reward for performing dharma and punishment for violating it"; purity and pollution "include both acquired pollution and inborn, inherent degrees of purity-pollution" (p.319).

As a social system, caste continually undergoes restructuring and redefinition (Berreman, 1979, p.105). Since social systems are the products of human interaction, Berreman asserts that "a social hierarchy is continually redefined, affirmed, challenged, and validated by interaction even as interaction is continually constrained by the hierarchy" (p.105-106).

Caste associations are reinforced by various institutions in Indian society. Berreman (1979) refers to castes as "kin-classes" which stratify South Asian peasant society. He notes that the kin component of caste in India is reinforced in economic, political, and religious institutions (p.318). Economically it is visible in the shared occupation within family and caste; politically it is seen in the caste panchayats (local governing councils); religiously caste is closely identified with Hinduism, as described above (*ibid*). Berreman states that caste associations provide "a mechanism for political or economic activity and status enhancement and comprise an interest group for people who, in their individual families and castes might be too few, too poor, or too powerless to achieve their ends" (p.231). Panchayats can help to negotiate the needs and interests of caste members with other social groups (*ibid*).

A central question which naturally emerges when considering caste structure is how and if the caste system will ever dissolve. Sukhadeo Thorat (2007) describes features of caste which make it a rigid institution. One such feature is that civil, cultural, religious, and economic rights are pre-determined or birth-ascribed, and Thorat states that the assignment of these rights is "unequal and hierarchical" (p.287).

Another feature which makes the caste system rigid is social ostracism, which is reinforced by Hindu philosophy (Thorat, 2007, p.288). Thorat also points out that castes cannot exist in isolation; they are interlinked as a system. Both Thorat (2007) and Ambedkar (1987) hold that the privileges and rights of higher castes leave lower castes with disabilities. Social and physical exclusion and isolation, for example, characterize the Untouchables (Thorat, 2007, p.289).

To sum up these points, the caste system in India gives individuals a unique birth-ascribed identity within hierarchically arranged social groups. Based on the literature on Dalits which follows, it is evident that caste is so imbedded in Indian society that it is unlikely to dissolve at any point in the distant future.

Dalits and 'Untouchability' in India

Dalits, formerly called the untouchables, are at the bottom of India's caste hierarchy. The term 'Dalit' is a self-chosen identity as a rejection of those identities which have been imposed upon the group. The NGO Navsarjan claims that Dalit is an empowering term, defined as those who "believe in equality of all humans, practice equality, and protest inequality" (Dalit Flyer, p.11, CITE). The literature shows, however, that Dalits are still subjected to discriminatory practices connected to untouchability.

The social manifestations of untouchability are deep-rooted. Shah *et al* (2006) write, "'Untouchability' is an extreme and particularly vicious aspect of the caste system that prescribes stringent social sanctions against members of castes located at the bottom of the purity-pollution scale" (p.21). Untouchable castes are considered separate from even the lowest castes of the hierarchy. Shah *et al* state, "they are considered to be so 'impure' that their mere touch severely pollutes members of all other castes, bringing terrible punishment for the former and forcing the latter to perform elaborate purification rituals" (*ibid*). The practice of untouchability involves not just the avoidance of physical touch but also broader social sanctions such as exclusion, subordination, and exploitation.

There is a certain circular logic which compounds the practice of untouchability. Dalits, as the lowest social class in India, are compelled to work in unclean occupations, namely those jobs associated with death or the removal of human and animal excrement. As Shah *et al* (2006) write, "The impurity of the task and the low status of those who perform it are mutually reinforcing characteristics; in the circular logic of untouchability, the tasks are 'impure' because they are performed by Dalits, and Dalits are impure because they perform these tasks" (p.106).

Many Dalits who work in these manual scavenging positions feel powerless to resist this humiliating work simply because alternative work is unavailable or not secure (p.110). Herein lies a great contradiction: for Dalits to escape work that involves scavenging or disposal of human carcases may lead to economic insecurity, but to remain in this occupation "they must accept the lowest depths of social degradation" (p.112).

One leader who tried to bring dignity to manual scavengers was the well-known Hindu activist, Mahatma Gahndi. He went to the extent of cleaning his own toilet in support of the Dalits, and later called for the abolition of manual scavenging (Shah *et a*l, p.109). The government has also banned the practice of manual scavenging, but there are still over one million Dalits working as scavengers in India today (Kumar, 2005). A 2002 survey revealed that 95% of these scavengers are women and girls (*ibid*).

Gandhi coined the term "harijan", or people of God, to give the untouchables a more honorable name. Abolishing untouchability was one of Gandhi's main social priorities, an endeavor he began around 1915 and supported until his death in 1948 (Kinsley, 1993). By interacting regularly with harijans in his community and while traveling, Gandhi demonstrated that they deserved to be treated as equals in Indian society. He strongly emphasized the importance of manual labor and self-sufficiency, no matter how lowly the task (p.104). Rao (2003) cites that Gandhi also framed untouchability as a caste issue which should be recognized by the Hindu community, who excluded harijans from Hindu worship (p.21).

Gandhi's efforts, along with others, led to greater awareness among government leaders of the untouchables' status. In 1935 the untouchable castes were put on a list, or "schedule" to receive benefit, hence the term "Scheduled Castes (SC)" emerged (Moon, 2001, p.xi). Furthermore, the Constitution of India (1950) made the practice of untouchability illegal, and in 1955 it was made punishable by law.

Despite his work to abolish untouchability, Gandhi is not held in high regard among the untouchables. One reason for this is that the term harijan was considered as patronizing to the "politically aware untouchables" (Moon, 2001, p.x). A second related issue is that Dr. Ambedkar, the most respected and well-known Dalit leader, encountered a major clash with Gandhi in 1932. Gandhi denied the untouchables "the right to political power that Dr. Ambedkar felt was essential for progress" (*ibid*).[2] For Ambedkar, political recognition of Dalits was the pressing issue, not their religious inclusion in Hindu society (Rao, 2005, p.22).

Ambedkar is considered the pioneer of the Dalit movement. A rare case for a Dalit, Ambedkar left India to earn a law degree and doctorate in the United States

---

[2] The Pune Pact of 1932 was an "agreement between Ambedkar and Gandhi in which Ambedkar gave up a separate electorate for untouchables that would have allowed them to elect their own representatives (as the Muslims did) and secured additional reserved places in the legislatures. The pact took place in the Yeravda Jail in Pune, where Gandhi was held, and was signed to prevent Gandhi's death by fasting" (Moon, 2001, p.184).

and England. He returned to India to become a strong political leader for Dalit liberation. He converted from Hinduism to Buddhism in 1956 and led many Dalits to abandon their Hindu roots (Ambedkar, 1990). Seenarine (2004) cites that Ambedkar was appointed as Law Minister for India's first independent government and had a strong influence on raising awareness about Hindu domination (p.36). Ambedkar used de-Hinduization, "an ancient form of resistance among Dalits" which involved a strong protest against Hinduim and willing acceptance of a non-Hindu religion (*ibid*).

The influence of Ambedkar sparked a strong movement among Dalits. With the Dalit movement came an ideological shift that involved treating the untouchables not as passive members of society but as empowered individuals. By 1970s the term 'Dalit' came into full use in movements such as 'Dalit Panthers' and 'Dalit literature' (Moon, 2001, p.xi). Dalit Panthers were a group of Dalit activists and writers who spoke out about discrimination from the slums of Bombay (Seenarine, 2004, p.36).

Ideological Shift

The term Dalit brought a strong political connotation. As Rawat (2006) states, "Dalits questioned and rejected categories like untouchables, Depressed Classes, Scheduled Castes, and Harijans that were coined by colonial and Hindu/nationalist discursive practices. This was not merely to contest dominant ascriptions of their identities but also, more importantly, to question the notions of impurity and pollution attached to their community, identity, and history" (p.1).

Two authors that highlight Dalits' agency in recognizing their oppression include Shah *et al* (2006) and Moon (2001). Shah *et al* (2006) write that a large number of Dalits see their status as a direct result of upper caste dominance and exploitation. Dalits have resisted such oppression from efforts ranging from passive resistance to militant retaliation (p.145).

Secondly, Vasant Moon's (2001) autobiography, *Growing up Untouchable in India*, describes his life growing up in the Mahar caste, an untouchable caste in Maharashtra. The introduction states: "In Moon's world, Dalits are not unhappy victims, not marginalized peoples to be pitied, not a people without hope. Prejudice, violence, crime are not absent from the story of his early life, but they do not dominate, do not destroy his spirit" (p.xi). The term Dalit is thus commonplace today to represent a sense of agency, not a passive acceptance of their fate.

Despite the progress that Dalits have made in raising awareness about their oppression, caste discrimination remains as a common reality in their everyday life. Article 15 of the Indian Constitution prohibits discrimination on grounds of religion, race, caste, sex, or place of birth. Furthermore, Article 17 states that "Untouchability is abolished and its practice in any form is forbidden.[3] The literature shows, however, that caste-based discrimination is still common throughout India for Dalits. Human Rights Watch (2007) states,

> The Government of India has not refrained from committing and supporting discriminatory acts against Dalits, and has failed to implement measures to end caste discrimination. India has failed to encourage integrationist

---

[3] Government of India (1950). http://indiacode.nic.in/coiweb/welcome.html

movements and has not provided for the development and protection of Dalits, who as a result remain an extremely marginalized social group.[4]

Human Rights Watch regularly reports discriminatory acts to make the government more accountable for their treatment of marginalized groups.

In 2006, Prime Minister Manmohand Singh compared Dalits' situation with apartheid. He said, "Even after 60 years of constitutional and legal protection and support, there is still social discrimination against Dalits in many parts of our country". He went on to say, "Dalits have faced a unique discrimination in our society that is fundamentally different from the problems of minority groups in general. The only parallel to the practice of untouchability was apartheid" (Rahman, 2006). By no surprise, Prime Minister Singh's words were spread across newspapers and journals worldwide. The caste system in India has remained a major social issue that is recognized around the globe. Rahman noted that this was the first time that an Indian leader compared the Dalit condition to that of South African apartheid (p.1).

There is an obvious tension social tension between Dalits who are fighting for their own emancipation versus social forces which relegate them to practices of untouchability. The literature alludes to ways in which Dalit women have worked towards freeing themselves from these social ills, which is highlighted in the next section.

---

[4] Human Rights Watch (2007): http://www.hrw.org/reports/2007/india0207/6.htm#_Toc158704453

Dalit Women

Dalit women have not been silent in the Dalit movement. Dr. Ambedkar's push to politically mobilize Dalits encouraged many women to actively participate as well. Moon and Pawar (2005) have documented women's participation in the untouchable movement. Their study shows that by 1930 women began to conduct their own untouchable meetings with the encouragement of Ambedkar. Women also participated in sit-ins in front of Hindu temples because they were denied access to them (p.50).

Moon and Pawar (2005) also cite that strong resolutions were passed by women in an untouchable conference in Bombay in 1936. The resolutions demanded the following: free and compulsory education for girls; women's representation in state legislative assemblies; training for self-protection of untouchable women; starting a women's wing in the Equality Volunteer Corps; prohibiting child marriages (p.51). These early initiatives demonstrate that even though Dalit men and women shared a similar oppression, Dalit women had their own specific agenda and needs which they wanted to be made known. Throughout the latter half of the 20th century, Dalit women continued to be active in the Dalit Movement.

Recent literature shows, however, that Dalit women remain as one of the most marginal groups in Indian society. Bandhu (2005) writes, "Many studies have documented in measurable and objective terms that Dalit women are in a worse-off position than Dalit men or non-Dalit women in terms of wages, employment, occupation and assets, education, health, social mobility, and political participation" (p.110).

Bandhu's statement about Dalit women's position can be supported by recent data from the National Campaign on Dalit Human Rights (NCDHR). According to the NCDHR website, out of India's 1.1 billion people, Dalit women comprise roughly 8% of the total population, or 80.5 million people. They make up 16% of the total female population and 48% of the Dalit population. The literacy rate of Dalit women compared to non-Dalit women is 23.8% and 39.3%, respectively. Comparing the poverty rate among these two groups reveals a similar trend, with a 36.2% poverty rate among Dalit women, compared to 21.6% among non-Dalit women.[5] It should be noted here is that tribal women in India are cited as being one of India's most vulnerable groups as well.

Additional data describe unemployment, literacy, and poverty rates among Dalit women. NCDHR cites:

> The unemployment rate of Dalit women is 4.0% against 0.97% among non-Dalits in rural areas and 3.3% against 1.98% for non-Dalits in urban areas. The literacy rate of Dalit women is just 23.8% compared to that of 39.3% among non-Dalits. Due to discrimination, poverty, and gender role ideology, Dalit women have a drop out rate of 53.96% at the primary school level. The poverty rate among Dalit women is 36.2% against 21.6% among non-Dalit women. 94% of Dalit women are engaged in the unorganized, self-employed sector (farm/wage workers, domestic helpers, etc.), marked by overwork, low wages, non-payment of equal wages, and absence of social security or maternity benefits.[6]

---

[5] Statistics taken from National Campaign on Dalit Human Rights (2006): http://www.ncdhr.org.in/ncdhr/campaigns/womensrights/.

[6] *Ibid*

Given this data, we can see that rural Dalit women face higher unemployment and poverty than non-Dalits and have a lower literacy rate.

Dalit women are also victims of sexual violence. The 2001 World Conference Against Racism highlights more specifically how Dalit women are affected by caste discrimination. A statement from the conference, the NGO Declaration on Gender and Racism, holds that Dalit women "face targeted violence from state actors and powerful members of dominant castes" (Rao, p.363). It states that Dalit women are subjected to unequal wages, violent discriminatory acts, and even rape and mutilation (*ibid*). What is even more astounding is that violence against Dalit women tends to go unreported.

The literature demonstrates that although Dalit women have been active in the Dalit movement, they remain highly vulnerable to poverty, violence, and caste discrimination.

Dalit Girls

Most literature dealing with female Dalits refers to 'Dalit women'. Given that childhood/adolescence represent a distinct life state from adulthood, attention needs to be given as to who Dalit girls are.

Seenarine's (2004) study, *Education and Empowerment Among Dalit Women in India: Voices from the Subaltern*, offers useful insight about the common characteristics of rural Dalit girls. In a study of 26 poor, rural Dalit girls, Seenarine found that child labor, education discrimination, and subordination were common characteristics. For the girls involved in the study, child labor involved mainly household production and wage work. Seenarine claims that their household and childcare roles are reinforced by patriarchal structures and gender indoctrination (p.67).

The second shared characteristic which Seenarine (2004) describes relates to free time and access to education. For some parents marriage takes precedence over education, so Dalit girls often drop out of school at an early age (p.68). In terms of self image, a study in Seenarine's book showed that "Dalit women accept a subordinate role to men and are submissive to the inequalities and injustices of marriage and family life" (p.69). Studies which go deeper into these issues will be explored in the next section.

Part II: Economic Status and Gender Discrimination

Economic Status

According to the literature, Dalits in general are among the most economically deprived groups in India. Shah *et al* (2006) highlight the blatant fact that caste hierarchy is reflected in economic status hierarchy of caste groups, especially in rural India (p.39). The National Campaign on Dalit Human Rights (2002) points out that Dalits have lower standards of housing quality and basic amenities.

Two points about economic status which emerge from the literature relate to hereditary occupation within the caste structure, while the second explores how child marriage affects Dalit girls' economic opportunities.

Seenarine (1996) points out that Dalits are not just a socio-cultural group but an economic class as well (p.2). He cites these startling statistics:

> The 1971 census figures show that over half of the Dalit workforce were landless agricultural laborers, compared to 26% of the non-Dalit workforce. A number of social studies have shown that Dalit women make up a large number of the professional sex workers. Studies reveal that 90% of those who die of starvation and attendant disease are Dalits (p.2).

The caste system often leads Dalits to pursue their hereditary occupation. For the upper castes their jobs in fields such as engineering, medicine, and law clearly require years of schooling and advanced education. Dalits, however, are born into occupations like scavenging, removing nightsoil, curing hides, preparing shoes, and removing animal carcasses (Jain *et al*, 1997). These low status positions make Dalits particularly vulnerable to poverty, as they require little education to perform such work, and many of these jobs plague Dalits with serious disease.

Many Dalit women become manual scavengers, and job characterized by intense physical and mental stress. The Report of the Occupational Health and Safety Center in Mumbai of 1996 (from NCDHR, 2002, p.33) offers statistics on manual scavenging. See Table 2.1.

Table 2.1 Health Statistics on Manual Scavenging

- 49.3% of scavengers examined had respiratory complaints
- 12.5% had skin diseases
- 55.9% had orthopedic complaints
- 7.2% had eye disease

Table 2.1 continued

• 26.3% had gastro intestinal problems • 11.8% suffered from weight loss • 12.5% suffered from mental stress and alcohol addiction

Source: NCDHR (2002, p.33)

In 1993 the government banned the construction of dry latrines and the employment of manual scavengers through the Employment of Manual Scavengers and Construction of Dry Latrines Prohibition Act (NCDHR, 2002, p.33).

Dalit women are cited by NCDHR (2002) as being perhaps the most economically deprived section of Indian society. The data in Table 2.2 support the claim.

Table 2.2 Economic Deprivation of Dalit Women.

Dalit women rarely own land; most work as daily wage agricultural laborers.
In rural India in 1991 around 71% of Dalit women workers were agricultural laborers and 19% were cultivators. This is contrasted with 43% of non-Dalit women as agricultural laborers and 42% cultivators.
Agricultural work is seasonal in nature and is available only at certain times, so that at other times there is no work and hence no income.
In rural and urban areas the unemployment rate among Dalit women is higher than the unemployment rate of non-SC/ST women.
The recent National Sample Survey shows that the unemployment rate of Dalit women on a current daily basis is 4.0% while it is less than 1% for non-SC/ST women.
Poverty levels of agricultural workers (mainly female) are as high as 60% for rural agricultural laborers and 73% for urban casual laborers.

Source: NCDHR (2002, p.29)

NCDHR (2002) also claims that Dalit women are "hapless victims of market forces", especially given that their concentration in the unskilled labor force (p.30). Another salient point from NCDHR is that Dalit women are unseen in the domestic sphere, where they have a heavy work burden and limited household resources (p.30).

In the case of Dalit women we can see the spectrum of economic employment ranging from that of manual scavenging to the success of Mayawati of the Bahujan Samaj Party. Mayawati, a Dalit woman, was elected the Chief Minister of Uttar Pradesh, the largest state in India (p.53). The reality for most Dalit women, however, is that they remain the poorest group in India, along with the Scheduled Tribes (Shah *et al*, 2006). With limited resources and lack of economic opportunities, Dalit women tend to inherit the impoverished lifestyles of their predecessors.

The second main point about economic status in the literature is that child marriage limits Dalit girls' ability to access economic opportunities in India. According to the International Center for Research on Women (ICRW, 2005), there are 51 million girls aged 17 or younger in developing countries (p.2). Young brides face many health risks, including malnutrition, maternal mortality, infant mortality, obstetric fistula, and HIV infection (p.4). Child marriage also causes girls to drop out of school at an early age. All of these consequences of child marriage limit girls' economic opportunities.

In India 50% of girls are married before the age of 18 (ICRW, 2007). Cited causes for child marriage globally include poverty, transfer of wealth, custom, protection, community bonds, and lack of schooling (p.3). In 2005, the government of India passed an act which allows children as young as 15 to marry by their own will, a move which enraged many who support child rights in the country (Carvalho, 2005).

In short, Dalit girls are likely to work at an early age, marry early, and remain in an impoverished position relative to other social groups in the country.

Gender Discrimination

Discrimination against women in India begins at childbirth for many. Daughters are viewed as economic burdens, while sons are expected to contribute to family wealth and carry their father's lineage (ICRW, 2006). There are frequently cases, both reported and unreported, of infant girls being abandoned by parents who only aspire to raise a son. The Times of India (2008), for example, highlighted one such incident in January 2008, where an infant girl was deserted on an Ahmedabad train (p.9).

More generally, the National Human Development Report (2001) documents discrimination against Indian women. The report states,

> Throughout her life cycle, women's dignity, self-esteem and emotional well-being are compromised for some less overt, but widespread form of discrimination such as personal confinement and restriction on mobility, particularly in rural areas; almost complete marginalization in the decision making process at the household level; responsibility for household work including looking after younger siblings; sexual abuse by the family members, even incest; childhood/forced marriage and verbal abuse. (p.106).

The literature makes it clear that women in general face discrimination both in the public and private sphere. The National Human Development Report (2002) further highlights how the girl child is affected by gender discrimination in family upbringing. The report says that discrimination is visible in terms of education opportunities, skill formation, and the amount of household work that the girl is expected to do (p.26). Once she is married, she is often the target of domestic violence, which often goes unreported (*ibid*).

Looking historically at gender discrimination, it was Dr. Ambedkar who noted that progress in Indian society would not be possible without improving women's status. Ambedkar's first scholarly paper, "Castes in India: Their Mechanism, Genesis, and Development", describes three historic practices that have oppressed women in India: sati, forced widowhood, and child marriage (Kumar, 2007). Ambedkar led Dalit women on the historic 'Mahad Satyagraha' protest for drinking water rights in 1927. He organized conferences which addressed women's issues exclusively for Dalits.

For Ambedkar, women's status would not be improved without giving them voice in the Dalit Movement (*ibid*).

Education Status

Due to their low social and economic status, Dalits are unlikely to finish school. According to the National Commission for SC and ST (2001), the national drop-out rate among Dalit children is 36.6% at primary, 59.4% at middle, and 73.1% at secondary level of education (Government of India, 2000-2001).

Dalits make up nearly 16% of the Indian population, and are found in all regions in India. More specifically, they are found in large percentages in Uttar Pradesh and Punjab in the north, West Bengal in the east, Tamil Nadu and Andra Pradesh in the south, and Rajasthan and Maharashtra in the west. In addition, nearly three-fourths of Dalits live in rural India (Shah *et al*, 2006, p.39). There is a gap between urban and rural literacy rates in India, which Table 2.3 demonstrates.

Table 2.3 Basic Literacy Rate of Dalits (%)

Dalits in All-India		Urban Dalits		Rural Dalits	
37.41		55.11		33.25	
M	F	M	F	M	F
49.91	23.75	66.60	42.29	45.94	19.46

M-male, F-female   Source: Government of India, 1991 Census

While the urban-rural phenomenon is not a real surprise, what is more pronounced is the gap between Dalit males and females in all three categories.

A study from the National Committee of Scheduled Castes documents more clearly the literacy gap between Dalit men and women. See Table 2.4..

Table 2.4 Literacy Trend from 1961-1991

Year	All-India			Scheduled Castes		
	M	F	Total	M	F	Total
1961	34.44	12.95	24.02	16.96	3.29	10.27
1971	39.45	18.72	29.46	22.36	6.44	14.67
1981	65.50	29.85	43.67	31.12	10.93	21.38
1991	64.13	39.29	52.21	49.91	23.76	37.41

Source: National Committee on SC (2002, p.44)

This table demonstrates that there has been a steady increase in growth rate of literacy for SCs, but a widening gap between male and female SCs. In addition, there has remained a significant gap in literacy between SCs and total population.

Education statistics by region raise many questions. UNICEF points out that in the states of Rajasthan, Uttar Pradesh, Bhiar, and Mizoram nearly 60% of girls dropped out of school before finishing the first five years of primary school.[7] In addition, Table 2.5 displays enrollment percentages by state for SCs in higher education.

Table 2.5 SC Student Enrollment in Higher Education 1995

State	Percentage Enrolled
Maharashtra	21.74
Uttar Pradesh	13.92
Tamil Nadu	9.04
Andhra Pradesh	7.68
Karnataka	7.63
Gujarat	6.80
West Bengal	5.06
All other states and union territories	<5

Source: National SCST (1996-1997, 1997-1998, p.77)

The data causes us to question the difference among states. Both social and political factors influencing such discrepancies is beyond the scope of this paper.

The education status of Dalit students is lower compared to other social groups. Dalit girls in particular continue to lag behind Dalit boys in literacy trends and in enrollment in school.

Part III: Strategies to Promote Dalit Girls' Education

The education of Dalit girls is an important educational issue in India. Retention rates of SC girls are substantially lower than that of non-SC girls (Govinda

---

[7] UNICEF website: http://www.unicef.org/india/children_1414.htm

& Bandyopudhyahy, 2007). In addition, discrimination based on caste, economic status, and gender is salient among this social group. These interrelated factors affect girls' access to educational opportunities. The policy of reservations and other government actions have helped to improve Dalit's access to education post-independence (Seenarine, 1996). These initiatives, however, fail to adequately address the deeper social impediments which render schooling impossible for many Dalit girls.

This section reviews literature related to major government policies and NGO advocacy initiatives which support Dalit girls' education.

History of Women's Education in India

Literature which shows the emergence of a national interest in girls' education in India dates back to pre-Independence (before 1947). Chanana (1994) claims that before India's independence women's education was strongly linked to women's family roles (p.37). According to Chanana's historical research, social and political reform efforts in the 1920s sparked a greater interest in issues related to women's status. In 1929 women were granted the right to vote, and in the same year a minimum marriage age was set at 14. During this period more young women started going to school. Quoting Chanana, "As more and more women received formal education, they became conscious of their problems and social status and sought amelioration of their situation" (p.38).

Four main change agents in British India included Christian missionaries, Indian social reformers, philanthropic foreigners interested in women's causes, and the British government. These change agents sought to improve the status of women by giving them an education what would enable them to be better wives and mothers (Chanana, 1994, p.40). Chanana's research highlights the fact that women's education became important before India's independence in 1947. In 1922, over 6.9 million boys and 1.4 million girls were enrolled in school, and by 1947 these numbers increased to 13.9 million and close to 4.3 million, respectively (p.40).

One education trend prior to independence was that women's education was largely privatized and confined to urban areas (p.41). It became clear early on that women's education involved higher investment. Chanana cites some of these investments: escorts were needed for girls who had to walk long distances to school; women teachers needed to be trained to meet increasing demands; scholarships were needed at incentives to poor parents (p.41). There was also a strong public opinion to make the curriculum more relevant for girls, especially at the secondary school level (p.51). Chanana notes that by the time the Constitution was written in the 1950, a major shift in thinking about women's status came about. Women's education no longer became focused on teaching skills to support their domestic roles, but "an instrument providing equality of opportunity for women" (p.54). In the next section, an analysis of major government policies linked to the education of women and Scheduled Caste women will be examined.

Major Government Policies

Table 2.6 highlights provisions in the Constitution for women and Scheduled Castes, as well as other government education policies related to these groups. It begins by noting key articles in the 1950 Constitution, followed by policies implemented through the National Policy of Education (NPE) of 1968 and 1986.

Table 2.6 Government Education Policies

Date	Action/Provision
1950	**Constitutional Articles**: Article 29(2): Protection of educational interests of minorities (on grounds of religion, race, caste, language). Article 46: Promotion of educational and economic interests of Scheduled Castes, Scheduled Tribes, and other weaker sections. (Constitution of India, 1950)
1986	**National Policy on Education** Point 4.1: Education for Quality Puts special emphasis on removal of disparities and equalizing access to those who have been denied education access. Point 4.2-4.3: Education for Women's Quality "Education will be used as an agent of basic change in the status of women" (p.8). Point 4.4-4.5: Education of Scheduled Castes Central focus on equalizing education development of SC's with non-SC's. Also scholarships scheme created for children of scavenging, flaying, and tanning families; careful monitoring of enrollment, retention, and completion rates; recruitment of SC teachers; provision of facilities to promote full participation of SC. (Government of India, 1998)
1989	**Scheduled Castes and Scheduled Tribes Act, 1989 (Prevention of Atrocities Act)** An act addressed at curbing violence against SC/ST which provides Special Court for trial against such offences. (Government of India, 1989)
1990	**Constitutional Establishment of National Commission for SC & ST** The NCSCST has extensive functions to prevent and protect both the welfare and development of SC/ST. (NCSC, 2004, p.1)

Table 2.6 continued

December 2002	**Constitutional Bill (86th Amendment)** Free compulsory schooling is named a fundamental right for all children aged 6-14. (Government of India, 2007, p.4)
September 2003	**National Program for Education of Girls at Elementary Level** Program aimed at "enhancing the provisions of under-privileged/disadvantaged girls at elementary level". Key components include community mobilization, development of model schools, gender sensitization of teachers and curriculum. (Government of India, 2007, p.5)
2004	**Kasturba Gandhi Balika Vidyalaya** Program sanctioning 1,180 residential schools to girls belonging to SC/ST and other backward castes. (Government of India, 2007, p.5-6).
February 2006	The Department of Women and Child development was elevated to the status of Ministry at the Union level. They have since published a major report, "A World Fit for Children", which analyzes children's issues at the national and state level. (Government of India, 2007, p.2)

The NPE 1968 sought to bring reconstruction to the education system, improve its quality, give greater attention to science and technology, and cultivate moral values (p.2). By 1986, the government attempted to provide stronger implementation for policies set out in the earlier NPE, as it did not adequately address problems of access, quality, quantity, utility, and finances. The 1986 NPE introduction states, "There are moments in history when a new direction has to be given to an age-old process. That moment is today" (p.2).

In addition to the provisions/actions highlighted in the table, state governments have also implemented their own schemes based on local needs. One example is in the state of Bihar, where the government has established 30 residential schools for SC boys, 21 schools for SC girls, and 15 for ST students (Government of India, 2007, p.6).

The extent to which the government has been successful at implementing policies that support Dalit girls' is highly questionable. Human Rights Watch holds the government accountable for its policies and often reports cases that have proved unsuccessful.

In terms of the Bihar residential schools, a human rights' report by Manthan (2000) clearly indicts the state for not meeting the basic right to education for SC. The report examines two girls' and two boys' residential schools in Bihar. The findings show a lack of minimum facilities in all four schools. The author of the report writes, "Though only four schools are presented in this case study, the situation of the schools is so dismal that one wonders if the government is in reality concerned at all with the educational welfare of Dalit children" (p.167). While the report is informative, it makes a strong assumption that the government is the only stakeholder to be held accountable for the dismal conditions of the Bihar schools.

As stated in the introduction of this paper, major social factors affect the government's ability to fully implement its policies aimed at supporting marginalized groups. At the grassroots, local, and national level, all groups should be held accountable for democratizing the education system to support all marginalized groups. The next section explores advocacy initiatives by NGOs and Dalit leader to support Dalit girls' education.

Advocacy Initiatives

Advocacy in this study refers to speaking on behalf of a group to raise awareness of a particular issue or cause. Three well-known advocates for Dalit rights in India include Navsarjan, Dalit Foundation, and Dalit Freedom Network. Descriptions of advocacy strategies of these three groups are listed below.

Navsarjan

Established in 1988, Navsarjan's mission is: "To eliminate discrimination based on caste and untouchability practices, to assure equality of status and opportunities for all, and ensure the rule of law". Its three guiding principles are as follows:

1. The violence on Dalits is a systemic phenomenon. It can only be countered through a very broad based organization.
2. The most crucial requirement in the movement is leadership, which must be stable as well as sensitive to its communities. This is best possible from the community within.
3. The war is more psychological than physical. There is a need therefore for mass awareness programs on a continued basis, along with action-oriented programs. Source: Navsarjan, "Navsarjan Biography", 2004

Besides monitoring cases of atrocities against Dalits and advocating for the ban of manual scavenging, Navsarjan operates four coeducational Dalit schools. Three primary schools are located in villages in Gujarat, which help students realize the correlation between education and Dalit empowerment.

Dalit Foundation

The Dalit Foundation is a registered trust that was established in 2003. It mission is "to be a partner in the struggle to eliminate caste-based discrimination and ensure equality and equal rights for all". Its four main objectives:

1. Eradicate untouchability, social discrimination, and caste-based atrocities, with special focus on Dalit women.
2. Provide support for livelihood – minimum wages, education, health, housing, and insurance for laborers in the unorganized sector.
3. Rights over land, water bodies, villages, forests and other means of production.
4. Create public understanding of favorable public opinion.

Source: Dalit Foundation, 2004, "Dalit Foundation – About Us".

The foundation offers grants to Dalit activists who raise awareness of caste-based discrimination, especially programs which focus on women. Most of its grants which support women's issues are based on eradicating manual scavenging.

In an interview with Anisha Chugh of the Dalit Foundation, she discussed the Dalit Foundation's focus on education. "We are just introducing a scholarship for young Dalit students who voice discrimination in schools", she said. Ms. Chugh spoke of discrimination in mid-day meals, where Dalit students are often not allowed to eat with other students in school, and some are even denied a meal altogether. "Caste discrimination is most pronounced at the mid-day meal, and students need to voice this injustice", she said. With its focus on eliminating discrimination in schools, the Dalit Foundation hopes that Dalit students can be treated with dignity in the classroom and mid-day meal. (Chugh, 2008)

Dalit Freedom Network

The Dalit Freedom Network's (DFN) mission is to empower Dalits in their quest for social freedom and human dignity by networking human, financial, and informational resources. It does this through four main programs: education, economic development, medical resourcing, and social justice. (Dalit Freedom Network, 2006)

In terms of its education focus, DFN places its emphasis on English-language schools. The aim in doing so is to bridge the gap between English-speaking Brahmins and illiterate Dalits. The All India Christian Council, a partner of DFN, runs 1,000 Dalit Education Centers in India for Dalit students. Each school provides primary education to approximately 250 students.

In an interview with Mr. Madhu Chandra of DFN in New Delhi, he spoke of English being a source of power for Dalit girls. He said, "Any Dalit student educated in English gains global power. To know what is going on in the world brings empowerment to Dalit families and communities" (Chandra, 2008). He said DFN in Delhi has a special focus on working with Dalit families to help them get girls in school. "We focus on education and empowerment with families", Chandra says. DFN thus works to build dignity in Dalit girls by providing them with an English-based education, one that their families are supportive of.

CEDAW

Besides the three organizations described above, issues surrounding Dalit women's rights have been raised by the Convention on the Elimination of All Forms of Discrimination against Women (CEDAW), an important international convention. Despite constitutional guarantees of equality for women, Dalit women face "age-old discrimination and prejudices that operate in multiple layers across class, regional, and geographic boundaries, conspiring to keep Dalit women in a position of dependence on political, social, and economic forces" (Stephen, 2007, p.37). Stephen writes that legislation banning manual scavenging, the prevention of atrocities against SCs and government reservations have not been effectively implemented (*ibid*).

Given ineffective legislation to support Dalit women, Stephen (2007) asserts that CEDAW has 3 main strengths which effectively promote Dalit women's rights. The strengths of CEDAW are described below:

1. It embodies the principle of state obligation by making the state accountable to its efforts to bring about an enhancement in the position of women and to provide equal opportunity in the areas of legal and judicial system, political participation and representation, decision-making, programs, and institutions.

2. It obligates states to bring domestic legislation to be in conformity with the principles of CEDAW.
3. It provides a comprehensive framework for the advancement of women and provides a framework for understanding the concept of equality: equality of opportunity and equality of results. (p.37).

In New York in January 2007, the CEDAW Committee raised several key questions and made recommendations on human rights violations concerning Dalit women and girls in India, such as trafficking for prostitution and the non-implementation of laws banning manual scavenging (*ibid*).

Conclusion

This chapter provided an overview of the Dalit population and major Government policies aimed to support the education and welfare of women and SC. Dalit girls, like other poor girls in India, tend to marry early and have limited economic and social opportunities. What has emerged in the literature, however, is that the Dalit movement has helped to support Dalit rights and encourage Dalits to resist caste oppression.

CHAPTER 3

METHODOLOGY

Methods

This study drew on informational interviews and analyses of scholarly literature and official government documents on Dalit issues. The methodology used is described in Table 3.1:

Table 3.1 Methodology

Objective	Method
To analyze the relationship between caste, economic status, and gender.	Analyze scholarly literature and official government documents.
To document what Dalit girls' say about discrimination against them.	Observe and interview 7 Dalit girls (aged 18-25) in their school, Dalit Shakti Kendra in Gujarat.
To document the extent to which Dalit girls see education as a means to overcome discrimination.	Observe and interview 7 Dalit girls (aged 18-25) in their school, Dalit Shakti Kendra in Gujarat.

The main documents analyzed included the Indian Census and National Policy of Education from various years, books and articles on Dalit studies by Berreman (1979), Kropac (2007), Seenarine (1996, 2004), and Thorat (2007), as well as reports from Dalit NGOs on Dalit girls. The documents were analyzed by synthesizing key points about the social and educational context that makes up Dalit girls everyday environment. In addition, historic literature was surveyed to understand how the Dalit Movement has shaped Dalit girls today.

In January 2008 the researcher spent seven days observing classes and meeting with Dalit girls at Dalit Shakti Kendra (DSK), a vocational education program run by the Navsarjan Trust in the state of Gujarat, India. The school is located in a village 25 kilometers outside of Ahmedabad, Gujarat. Dalit girls were asked questions related to their education and social background. After the interviews, the stories were compiled, and major cross-cutting themes about the girls' educational and social opportunities were analyzed.

Participant Selection

The researcher conducted seven interviews with Dalit girls at Dalit Shakti Kendra (DSK) in Gujarat. Girls selected for the interview were chosen from sixty girls enrolled in DSK's vocational education courses. After initially talking with about fifteen of the girls at DSK, the researcher selected seven based on varied educational and family backgrounds. The young women interviewed were aged 17-30. The researcher originally intended to interview young women aged 17-25, but also included the eldest female at the school, a 30-year old with a unique family history.

Background of DSK

The vocational training school was founded in 2000 by Navsarjan, a Dalit organization which focuses on fighting caste-based discrimination in Gujarat. The school's main leaders, Martin Macwan and Manjula Pradeep, are Dalit and have a strong presence at the school. Macwan leads an evening prayer with students, and coordinates training workshops on relevant Dalit issues, such constitutional rights and the status of the Women's Movement. Manjula Pradeep is Director of Navsarjan and she is the main administrator at DSK.

Table 3.2 shows the concerns, objectives, and programs associated with DSK.

Table 3.2 DSK's Objectives and Programs

Concern	Objective	Program
1. Caste society does not provide free space to the discriminated, where the youth can grow in healthy personalities.	Provide free space to you where they can grow as persons with skills and dignity.	Personality development inputs.
2. Youth are trapped into caste-based occupations as the major source of economic activity.	Elimination of dependence on caste-based occupations and stepping into self-employment sector.	Vocational training.
3. To be the oppressors-like is seen as the sole model for liberation from oppression.	Challenge the internalization of hierarchical values of caste system.	Social and political consciousness through value education.
4. Loss of motivation and increased frustration among youth.	Motivate youth for positive action.	Understanding self in the mirror of self-reflection and spirituality.
5. Both society and community do not provide free space for Dalit women for their growth as equals.	Ensure higher representations of DSK at all levels.	Raising consciousness and awareness about their rights along with vocational training.

Source: Dalit Shakti Kendra (2004). "The Power of Equality in Practice". DSK Bulletin. Ahmedabad: Dalit Shakti Kendra.

While Navsarjan has a focus on the empowerment of Dalit women, its focus at DSK is not segregated by gender. Both Martin Macwan and Manjula Pradeep believe that DSK should focus on Dalit students as a whole (Macwan, 2008).

Kropac (2007) describes the vocational basis of the school. "The main goal is to teach the students marketable skills that break through the caste system and its division of occupation. Occupations such as tailoring or carpentry are caste-based vocations of non-Dalits being offered at the center, but also occupations not rooted in the caste system are taught, like Video and Photography" (p.30). Students applying for a course are only required to able to read and write; DSK wants to give school drop-outs greater opportunity to learn a vocation (*ibid*).

The school also focuses on personality building and social consciousness. Kropac (2007) writes, "Before Dalits can morally demand to be treated as equals to other castes, they need to treat all Dalits as equals as well, across caste and gender lines" (p.30). Self-confidence, self-respect, and discipline are values taught at the school through evening prayer sessions and Sunday workshops. Dalit students are also required to clean their own bathrooms, wash their own clothes and dishes, and they are required to pay the full course fee of 200 rupees per month (approximately $6). DSK thus has a dual function – to teach students marketable skills for the unorganized sector and to offer them skills to be financially independent (*ibid*).

The Courses at DSK

The young women were enrolled in various vocational courses, including computers, tailoring, and beautician. Two of the seven interviewed were former DSK students who stayed on to become teachers, one in tailoring and the other in video/photography. Table 3.3 lists the courses available at DSK.

Table 3.3 Enrollment in DSK Vocational Courses as of 2007

Course	Male	Female
Mobile repair	35	3
Beautician	1	37
Police/security services	118	19
Furniture	96	0
Fabrication	38	0
Motor rewinding	106	0
Electrician	54	1
Machinist	15	0
Auto mechanic	193	0
Driving	286	5
Tailoring industrial	11	2
Tailoring (gents)	312	2
Tailoring (ladies)	3	476
Textile designing	34	56
Screen printing	1	1
Basic computer	130	65
Computer tally	7	2
Video/photography	47	6

Source: DSK School Data, 2008

One of the Dalit teachers interviewed has actually taken three DSK courses. She said she was so excited by how much she learned through her first DSK course, tailoring, that she decided to also take textile design and photography. All of the other girls have taken one course.

The courses that the girls enrolled in were predominantly female, and all had Dalit teachers. The tailoring and beautician courses were taught by Dalit women while computers was taught by a Dalit man. Students begin their day with physical fitness at 6:00am, and they have class from 8:00am until 5:00pm. After two hours of free time, they attend a 30-minute prayer session and then have dinner.

Interviews

Hancock and Algozzine (1996) describe four variations in interview instrumentation. These variations include interview as informal conversation, guided conversation, open-ended responses, and as fixed responses (p.43). The researcher intends to use interview as a guided conversation, meaning that a few main questions will be pre-determined. This approach will be used in order to avoid having an overly-structured, formal interview with the Dalit girls and NGO leaders. The goal is to have a natural, fluid conversation. This approach also lends itself to making "data collection more systemic for each participant" (p.43).

Besides the interviews in Gujarat, additional data was gathered through informational interviews with persons associated with the Dalit Foundation and Dalit Freedom Network (DFN) They took place in Delhi in January. The Dalit Foundation is a grass-roots organization that advocates on topics such as Dalit women, education, health, and agriculture. Dalit men and women are awarded grants through the foundation to do research and advocate for Dalit issues. The Dalit Freedom

Network works to empower Dalits through education, economic development, medical resourcign, and social justice programs (Dalit Freedom Network, 2006).

During the seven interviews, the researcher met one on one with each girl, along with the translator. The conversations lasted approximately thirty minutes, though the longest one lasted for an hour. Guided questions used to begin the conversation included the following:

1. Which course are you taking at DSK?
2. What were you doing before you came to DSK?
3. What do you enjoy most about DSK?
4. What have been some of your interests in school?

Though these are very basic questions, the researcher wanted to leave the conversation open-ended to allow space for the girls to bring up other issues relevant to them.

Observation

Girls participated in vocational classes from 8:00am through 5:00pm. The researcher observed girls in tailoring, textile design, computers, beautician, and English class (a supplemental class). Informal observations were conducted to better understand the learning environment in which the girls are currently in.

Method of Analysis

Following the interviews and observations the data was analyzed. Initial impressions were recorded prior to the interviews, based on participant observation and initial encounters with the girls. After the interviews were conducted and basic anecdotes written, the researcher developed themes from the data. These themes were then used to substantiate conclusions and recommendations for further study.

Researcher Bias

With prior experience working in India, the researcher had a special interest in the study of caste and gender in India. She worked as a teacher in northern India from 2004-2005 in an international boarding school in the Himalayas. In addition, she participated in service learning activities with her students which brought her into close contact with orphaned children and the urban poor. Her experiences showed her stark contrasts among economic and social disparities among caste groups in India.

The researcher has also had a long-term interest in girls' education. Both in her past coursework and in an internship, she explored strategies to promote girls' education in regions such as the Middle East and Sub-Saharan Africa. Her prior research looked at ways to advocate for girls' education, to raise awareness at local and national levels.

With these past experiences in mind, the researcher had to be aware of bias that she would bring to this study. When conducting interviews, she tried to avoid asking leading questions and generating stereotypes.

CHAPTER 4

RESULTS AND DISCUSSION

This study seeks to address the following questions:

1. How do caste, economic status, and gender interrelate?

2. What do Dalit girls have to say about discrimination against them?

3. To what extent do Dalit girls see education as helping them to overcome discrimination?

These questions were examined through a qualitative approach which involved a review of scholarly literature and informational interviews with Dalit girls and leaders in Gujarat and New Delhi, India. The results of the research are discussed below.

Interrelatedness of Caste, Economic Status, and Gender

The literature does not treat caste, economic status (referred to as class as well), and gender as separate issues. Kropac (2007), Webster (2007), and Shah *et al* (2006) show in their analyses of Indian society the strong interplay among caste and economic status. In addition, Kumar (2007), Dube (2005), and Rao (2005) write about the overlap between caste, gender, and economic opportunity.

Caste division in Indian society is based both on the Varna and Jati systems. Its four-fold hierarchy through the Varna system has its roots in Hinduism. Brahmans (the priestly caste), Kshatriyas (the warrior caste), Vaishyas (the trading caste), and Shudras (the servile caste), form this basic hierarchical system. Caste also is described as being rooted in a more complex Jati system. Kropac (2007) points out that nearly 4,693 Jatis (sub-castes) exist in India today (p.7). Jatis are closely associated with one's traditional occupation and the group into which one is born (Kinsley, 1993, p.188).

Purity-pollution is a distinct characteristic of the caste system, which attributes one's social status as being pure or polluted simply by birth. Pure status is associated with higher castes while Dalits are considered the most impure for their polluting work, such as manual scavenging work. Kropac (2007) describes Dalits as having impure status, but it depends on the Jati to which one belongs. He writes, "Leather-making is still judged as a very 'impure' occupation, but it is slightly less 'impure' than sweeping floors" (p.8). In a hierarchical system based on Jatis, then, caste and economic status are almost interchangeable.

Similarly, one major point which emerged through Webster's (2007) analysis of Dalits is the connection of caste to economic status. He points out scholars have analyzed Dalits from two main approaches: class analysis and caste analysis. Using a class analysis, they consider the occupation status of Dalits, who work as peasants, agricultural laborers, and factory workers, among other jobs (p.76). Dalit scholars also use a "communal analysis of caste", and thereby focus on the Hindu notions of purity and pollution in inherent in the system (p.77). While some scholars may prefer an analysis based solely on caste, they undoubtedly find that Dalits' status in society is complexly linked to economic ties as well.

Shah *et al* (2006) state that over the past 100 years, rich and poor people are found in every class in Indian society. At the macro level, however, they assert that high economic status still characterizes upper castes, while low economic status characterizes lower castes (p.20). In short, caste hierarchy continues to reproduce economic status hierarchy in India.

Looking more specifically at gender, Dr. Ambedkar stated that gender could not be seen in isolation from caste (Kumar, 2007). According to Kumar, Ambedkar "clearly underlined that the caste system could be maintained only through control on women's sexuality" and that "women's subordination is located in their being the gateways to the caste system" (p.27).

In a similar way, Dube (2005) notes that caste has material bases given the unequal distribution of resources within the system. This has strong implications for gender and economic relations, as family units in lower castes tend to have restricted resources (p.224). Furthermore, in summarizing literature on Dalit women's subjugation, Rao (2005) writes,

> Caste relations are embedded in Dalit women's profound unequal access to resources of basic survival such as water and sanitation facilities, as well as to educational institutions, public places, and sites of religious worship. On the other hand, the material impoverishment of Dalits and their political disenfranchisement perpetuate the symbolic structures of untouchability (p.11)

Dalit women lack basic entitlements because they are women, Dalit, and poor.

To summarize, an analysis of the literature shows that social interactions create a strong interplay among caste, economic status, gender, and other factors. All of these factors can help us to understand Dalit girls' social reality in India.

Anecdotes from Interviews with Dalit Girls

The following seven anecdotes are from interviews with Dalit girls at Dalit Shakti Kendra in January 2008. Pseudonyms are used to hide the girls' identities.

Ganga

Ganga is a small, quiet girl, aged 17, in the tailoring course at DSK. She is an orphan. "My parents died when I was very young. I do not know exactly when or how they died. I have no memory of them", she said. Ganga completed school through fourth standard. She was then expected to take care of her household. Ganga has four older brothers, and she cooks and cleans for them regularly. She shared stories of being sexually abused by her brothers at home and never encouraged to return to school.

Ganga plans to work from home after she finishes at DSK. "I will do tailoring from home, and still care for my family", she stated. When asked how she will find work while in her home Ganga said, "I am learning how to make the sari blouse in my course and can make blouses for women in my community". She seemed excited to be able to work from home.

Indira

Indira, aged 26, was raised in the prosperous Annan district of Gujarat. She explained that the area is well-developed and known across India for its dairy farms. She went to school through tenth standard. Prior to joining DSK, Indira had no idea what the term "Dalit" really meant. "I always sat at the front of the class, did well in school, and had friends from higher castes", she said. She never made a distinction between caste groups. Once she learned more about Dalit history, Indira was shocked to learn about discrimination against Dalits.

Although Indira did not feel discriminated against in school, she said that her home situation was frightening. Her father never let her make decisions for herself. "He made me feel incapable of living my own life. I could not make any decisions without his support", she said. Her father threatened her often if she did not follow his wishes.

Indira always wanted to be a singer, but her father refused to let her pursue her dream. He wanted her to do work that would provide a steady income. Indira's father was supportive of her decision to enroll in the tailoring course at DSK in 2003. She liked the course so much that she decided to take three additional courses at DSK, and eventually she became the video and photography teacher at the school.

Indira did not expect to learn as much about her own identity as she did while studying and working at DSK. Her greatest mentor at DSK has been Martin Macwan, who she considers to be a "grandfather and godfather" in her life. "Martin knows all my pains", she says. He will draw pictures to represent what Indira is describing, and asks her to explain. "Why are you crying? You have ambition, right? What can you do to make your own decisions? Why does your father have power over you?" he would ask. These are just some of the questions that Martin frequently raised, which helped Indira to see her life from a new perspective.

Jwala

Jwala, aged 27, is from the scavenging community. She has worked at DSK since 2003. She is quiet and reserved, yet authoritative in the classroom. Jwala said that she would rather forget her school experience. She finished tenth standard, and admits that she was glad to be done with school. When she was ten years old her sister accidentally bumped into her teacher in the classroom. Her sister was publicly humiliated; she was scolded for her bad behavior. As an untouchable she was never supposed to come into contact with someone from an upper caste. Jwala quickly learned to avoid any interaction with her teachers.

"Scavengers are especially known in school and the community as the untouchables", Jwala said. She and her sister were never allowed to take water from the well in her village unless someone filled her jug. Once she touched the water tap and was scolded severely. "Scavengers are known", she repeated. "I have many stories about discrimination against my people".

Jwala came to DSK in 2003 to take the tailoring course. She wanted to find work outside of scavenging. After taking the course, Jwala stayed on to co-teach tailoring at DSK. "Teaching is very difficult, but satisfying", she told me. For

Jwala, she has found DSK to be the only school community that has ever accepted her.

Nandina

Nandina is 30 years old, and the eldest of all the students enrolled at DSK this term. She is in the computer course. Nandina's parents are both employed at a construction site in Surenagar. She has five siblings, none of whom have gone to school beyond tenth standard. Nandina is proud that she had the motivation to continue school through twelfth standard. "I didn't pass twelfth standard, but I studied hard and I'm glad that I got as far as I did", she said. When asked what motivated her to keep going to school, Nandina stated that she simply loves to learn. She also thinks that education made her more confident.

While Nandina spoke with a smile when talking about her success in school, her expression hardened when she spoke of a difficult marriage. She described the story: "I married someone I had never seen before. My father arranged it. We had one son. My husband brutally beat me; he smashed my face with a hammer and tried to kill me. I escaped with my son". Nandina showed the scars on her face; one above her eyebrow, one on her cheek, the other near her mouth.

After Nandina filed for divorce, she married another man. The problem is that the divorce never went through, leaving her socially ostracized for having two husbands. Nandina left her second husband to avoid this humiliation. "I smile and laugh now to forget such pain", Nandina said.

Nandina has worked for the last few years with the Self Employed Women's Association, known as SEWA. She has been a trainer with microfinance/self-help groups. She plans to use the computer skills she learns at DSK as she continues her SEWA job. Nandina commented that SEWA is a place where she has discovered a new purpose in life, which is to help other women who are struggling.

Nesreen

Nesreen identifies herself as a Muslim Dalit. She is 17 years old and her parents are from Pakistan. After seventh standard, Nesreen dropped out of school, which she says is common for Muslim girls. "Muslim girls are not expected to study past seventh standard. Girls hit puberty and then get married. I think 90% of Muslim girls under 18 are married in India. We have no choice", Nesreen declared angrily.

Nesreen married after she finished seventh standard, but the marriage did not last long. She married a man much older than her, and stayed only ten days with him and her in-laws before leaving. They eventually divorced. "I hate men. They use us. I will never marry again", she stated bluntly.

As a Muslim Dalit, Nesreen says that she can make few choices. She has no right to choose when to stop going to school, when to marry, and she stated, "I have no right to love". A second marriage is out of the question for Nesreen because she won't be forced to love someone.

Over the last few years, Nesreen has been employed at Aurocare Pharmaceutical Company. She worked in the production line, and was promoted to work with computers. She came to DSK this month to take a computer course for her new Aurocare position. Her favorite part of being a DSK student is learning about her rights as a Dalit woman and meeting other Dalit students.

Radha

Radha, aged 22, comes from a poor family in the Surendranagar District of Gujarat. Her father is a fieldworker and her mother stays at home. "My father is deaf and dumb, my mother is crippled. There is no breadwinner in my family", Radha declared frankly. The eldest of three daughters, Radha also has two brothers.

As a Dalit, Radha had reservation that gave her free hostal for primary and secondary school. With disappointment she shared her inability to finish tenth standard. "I failed tenth standard and could not continue. I could not finish my schooling if I failed a grade. I was sad that I could not move on", she stated. Despite this disappointment, Radha has a strong self-esteem. "Let the world say what it will about me. I'm a good person. I'm good to others and to my community. That's what's important", she asserted with confidence.

Without being able to continue with school, Radha began working in the fields. Though the work is very difficult, Radha said she feels obligated to help support her family financially, especially since she is the eldest daughter. In winter 2008, Radha had saved up enough money to enroll in DSK's beautician course. She did this for two reasons. For one, it would enable her to make more money for her family. She also admitted that she could "buy time" as a student. While she went through a formal wedding ceremony recently and is legally married now, she is not prepared to live with her husband and in-laws just yet.

Radha plans to finish the 45-day course, work a few more months to earn money for her family, and then return to her husband. When asked what she enjoyed most about her time at DSK so far, Radha said she likes talking with other girls in her course. "I am not excited about going back with my husband", she admitted.

Saroj

Saroj, age 22, completed her BA in Hindi and is proud to say that she's always been a good student. Her parents were always supportive of her education. Saroj's father was an accountant before he passed away during Saroj's junior year of college. Her mother is a housewife. Her family lives in the Ahmedabad District.

Saroj married in 2004 but because her family did not pay a sufficient dowry, her in-laws immediately threw Saroj out of the house. Her life took other unexpected turns. Saroj was in an accident which she chose to not describe in detail, but said that it left her with a fractured spine. She never fully recuperated from the accident and lost strength in her arms and bck. Since she was doing factory work at the time for INTS, a pharmaceutical company, she ended up losing her job because of her disability. Saroj had worked four years at the factory and was very unhappy when she had to leave because of her back problem.

After losing her job and being denied by her new family, Saroj moved back in with her mother and brothers. "My dream is to find a job", Saroj said. "I don't want to be dependent on others. I want to be independent". A family friend recommended DSK to Saroj, knowing that with her back problems she could not do any strenuous work. The very cheerful Saroj is enjoying her computer class. She hopes to find a computer job and earn money to support herself.

What do Dalit girls say about discrimination against them?

Of the seven girls interviewed, six shared stories about discrimination that they've faced. Table 4.1 lists the form of discrimination for each girl interviewed. This summary of main points is taken from the preceding anecdotes.

Table 4.1 Forms of Discrimination against Dalit Girls Interviewed

Interviewee	Form of Discrimination
Ganga	Sexual abuse by her brothers; encouraged to work at home at the age of ten rather than go to school.
Indira	Her father made her feel incapable of making her own life decisions and threatened her if she went against his wishes.
Jwala	She was emotionally abused and socially ostracized as a manual scavenger, especially at school and in her village.
Nandina	She was physically abused in her marriage.
Nesreen	As a Muslim Dalit her family and community did not allow her to make choices; not encouraged to go to school past seventh standard.
Radha	Not reported.
Saroj	Lost job because of physical disability from accident.

Four of the girls, Ganga, Indira, Nandina, and Nesreen shared stories about gender discrimination and physical or emotional abuse because they are female. Jwala faced social ostracism which she attributed to her status as an untouchable. Saroj, who had a crippling back injury, was unable to find work because of her physical condition. This is not necessarily discrimination; her accident limited her fully function physically.

The girls interviewed spoke often of discrimination in school, and the need for their own voices to overcome it. Jwala talked about blatant harassment in school, especially given her scavenging background. Nesreen spoke of her double burden of humiliation, because she is both Muslim and Dalit. She mentioned being humiliated often by boys at school because she is a Muslim Dalit. Given DSK's strong focus on speaking out against injustice, it comes as no surprise that the girls are eager to raise awareness about such discrimination.

To What Extent does Education help Dalit Girls Overcome Discrimination?

Table 4.2 lists the role that education has played to help the girls interviewed overcome discrimination.

Table 4.2 Role of Education to Overcome Discrimination

Interviewee	Role of Education to Overcome Discrimination
Ganga	Ganga hopes tailoring will help her economically when she returns home; she wants to work as a tailor from home.
Indira	Education (especially influence of Martin Macwan) at DSK taught Indira about her identity, which helped her to see that she has ambition.
Jwala	Education led Jwala to move out of the scavenging position and into teaching; she reported that she was accepted by her peers and teachers at DSK.
Nandina	School raised her self-confidence; a great place to make friends with other Dalits girls.
Nesreen	She learned about her rights as a Dalit at DSK.

Table 4.2 continued

Radha	Though she did not talk of discrimination, she said education would help her to be more secure economically because it would enable her to find work.
Saroj	She hopes that the computer course will enable her to find a job; given her back problem she can no longer do physical labor.

Ganga, Jwala, Radha, and Saroj all spoke of education as a means to economic opportunity; they directly linked their current coursework at DSK as a link to finding work. Both Indira and Nesreen stated that education helped them to learn about their identity and rights; it gave them greater consciousness as to who they are as Dalits. For Nandina, school provides a social opportunity; it boosted her self confidence and enabled her to make more friends.

In Chapter 5 these results will be discussed.

CHAPTER 5

CONCLUSIONS

To summarize the results of the research, caste, economic status, and gender are not treated as separate issues in the literature related to Dalit studies. Because of caste's strong association with occupation, it is difficult to isolate economic status from caste status. Additionally, gender is a cross-cutting theme in Dalit studies, especially given that India has a strong patriarchal society. Other key points which emerged from the research are presented below.

Discrimination against Dalit Girls

In an interview with seven Dalit girls at DSK, six girls spoke of discrimination against them. A majority of the girls faced gender discrimination; Ganga had been abused by her brothers for years, Indira's father prohibited her from making life decisions, Nandina was nearly killed by her husband in her home, and Nesreen's Muslim family forced her to quit school and marry in seventh grade. Only Jwala, the tailoring teacher at DSK who was formerly a manual scavenger, talked explicitly about caste discrimination as an untouchable.

While the literature shows a strong interconnectedness among caste, economic status, and gender, the girls interviewed revealed that gender discrimination affected them more frequently than economic or caste discrimination.

Pillai-Vetschera (2007) writes, "A Dalit patriarchy has developed in which Dalit men use the same mechanisms to subjugate their women as high-caste men had done for ages against their own women and also against the Dalits" (p.257). Not only do Dalit girls face gender discrimination in the public sphere, but they are confronted with it in their very own homes as well.

Role of Education

In terms of education's role to help the girls overcome this discrimination, we can conclude that education helped the girls interviewed to overcome economic hardship. Four out of seven girls said that education offered them more economic opportunities. Given that DSK is a vocational school, it is no surprise that the girls linked their education to economic opportunities.

Two girls interviewed spoke of the importance of learning about their Dalit identity in school. Again, DSK has a strong component of social consciousness raising, so the very nature of the school could have influenced their answers. We cannot make any generalizations from the interviews about whether education can help Dalit girls to overcome caste and gender discrimination. Ganga, Indira, Jwala, Nandina, and Nesreen shared stories about caste and gender discrimination but did not necessarily overcome it by going to school. In fact, Nesreen and Jwala faced harsh discrimination in school as a Muslim Dalit and manual scavenger; for them education may have increased the amount of discrimination they faced.

DSK's Focus on Fighting Discrimination

We can generalize when looking more broadly at DSK as a school that students educated there have the opportunity to overcome discrimination. Dalit girls are encouraged to protest injustice and learn more about their identity. Martin Macwan teaches students to fight discrimination in their homes and schools. He is also a strong advocate of eliminating gender-bias in school curricula.

Kropac (2007) writes, "Measures to raise self-confidence, self-respect, discipline, and social awareness are an important part of the DSK training. Students are taught that everyone has equal rights – women and men, people form all castes as well as Dalits and non-Dalits" (p.81). An impact study at DSK showed that nearly 57% of student respondents wrote that their relationship to other Dalits improved during the training. Also nearly 33% of Dalits believed that they have changed their attitudes and behaviors towards Dominant Castes (p.83). DSK may thus be a prime example of a school atmosphere which can help to eliminate caste and gender discrimination in school.

The DSK model may not be transferable. Kropac (2007) states that Navsarjan aims to improve the condition of Dalits in Guajarat; the organization provides flexible, short-term vocational training that may not be transferable to all markets (p.89). In any case, DSK's focus on Dalit empowerment and equality is an example of an effective approach to overcoming discrimination for this specific Dalit population.

Choice

One surprise in this study was the amount of choice the girls have in making decisions about their lives. Table 5.1 shows major choices the girls have been able to make.

Table 5.1 Major Choices Made by Girls Interviewed

Interviewee	Choice
Ganga	As an orphan and the only daughter among four children, Ganga has taken care of her brothers since she was a young girl. She dropped out of school after completing fourth standard, but made the decision at age 17 to learn tailoring so she could make money to care for her family.
Indira	She had an option for work immediately after finishing her 3 DSK courses – to teach at DSK – and she chose to stay.
Jwala	Jwala broke away from the scavenging community by saving money to come to DSK and take the tailoring course. She now is teaching tailoring at DSK.
Nandina	Nandina chose to leave her husband, get a divorce, and work with SEWA, a place where she enjoys helping poor women.
Nesreen	As a 17 year old Muslim Dalit, Nesreen has made the choice to never get married. She married at the age of 12, divorced, and has dreamed of going back to school since then. She now is taking a computer course at DSK.
Radha	She married a few months ago, and was uncomfortable living with her husband's family. One reason she chose to take the beautician class at DSK is to "buy time" before settling permanently with her new family.
Saroj	Even though she lost her factory job because of a chronic back injury, she redirected her career steps and decided to learn computers, with the hope to find a job where she does not have to stand.

These findings suggest that Dalit girls are able to make important choices in their lives in regards to their family, work, and education. This does not mean that they are free to make whatever choices they please; Nesreen clearly shows that Muslim

Dalits are often forced into marriage at an early age rather than being encouraged to go to school, and Jwala's narrative demonstrates that manual scavengers face harsh discrimination which limits their social opportunities.

The theme of choice, however, shows that Dalit girls are not necessarily stuck in their low social position. Some of the key elements which have helped the girls make positive life choices include parental support, personal motivation, and education. Indira and Saroj's stories, for example, reveal how important education has been for them to learn about their identity and pursue meaningful work opportunities.

Poverty

Poverty was another theme which emerged in the interviews. The relative socio-economic deprivation that Dalit girls face in comparison to other social groups in India cannot be ignored. Many girls risk repeating the cycle of poverty that their parents faced. A major challenge in encouraging girls to go to school rather than work in the fields or their households is that it often complicates their economic situation. Orphaned children like Ganga or those who live with only one parent may literally starve if they do not have some source of income to help their families. When weighing the alternatives of working versus going to school, many girls must opt to work to survive.

Advocacy Strategies

Two forces are at play in terms of discrimination against Dalit girls: family and society. For Nesreen, the Muslim Dalit, she faced pressure from her family to marry young and drop out of school. She was also socially ostracized in her school for being Muslim and Dalit. NGOs who advocate for Dalit rights should encourage parents to send their girls to school. More research needs to be done on how Dalit girls might overcome patriarchal forces in the public and private sphere.

The literature suggested that Navsarjan, the Dalit Foundation, and the Dalit Freedom Network all focus on Dalit rights and do some advocacy for Dalit education. It is important to consider how their current advocacy work addresses discrimination against Dalit girls. Table 5.2 summarizes their advocacy strategies.

Table 5.2 Advocacy Strategies of Dalit Organizations

Organization	Advocacy Strategy
Navsarjan	Focus on Dalit leadership; raise awareness about Dalit identity among individuals; promote continued self-reflection; make discrimination known to the public by reporting atrocity cases and gaining media attention.
Dalit Foundation	Make discrimination known to the public by encouraging Dalits to speak out against their own oppression.
Dalit Freedom Network	Educate Dalit girls in English-medium school; empower families to send girls to school.

There is broad advocacy for Dalit social rights, especially in terms of fighting caste and gender-based discrimination. As we can see, some of these strategies are directed at parents.

Recommendations

Based on the interviews with the seven Dalit girls, raising parents' awareness of the importance of their daughters' education is necessary since a majority of the girls faced gender discrimination on a regular basis. India is no doubt a strong patriarchal society. Navsarjan, Dalit Foundation, and Dalit Freedom Network all focus on fighting discrimination, but should have a greater focus on gender discrimination that takes place at the household level in order to promote girls' education.

On another note, the Government of India should not be blind to the social effects of discrimination against Dalit girls. Government education policies do consider discrimination against Dalits as a modern day issues, but need to carefully reflect the needs of Dalit girls in all stages of policy formation.

Without a doubt, DSK's model of raising Dalit consciousness offers students the opportunity to understand discrimination and oppression. In order for caste and gender injustice to be fully addressed, Dalit girls must also be given the voice to speak out against discrimination. An impact study should be done to better understand this aspect of DSK's vocational program.

Vocational training is an effective educational option for Dalit girls to overcome economic discrimination. DSK is a successful system to improve the economic status of Dalit girls in Gujarat. Kropac's (2007) impact study of DSK's vocational program showed that short-term training vocational training gives graduates a competitive advantage on the local labor market (p.85). Dalit girls in public schools in India should be given the opportunity to learn more about vocational training and its benefits for their future careers.

Concluding Remarks

Dalit girls interviewed at DSK indicated multiple times that they had agency in choosing their life direction. In each interview, girls brought up challenging aspects of their past, including domestic violence, divorce, discrimination in their villages, and lack of support from their families for school. At the same time, they described work and education as meaningful aspects of their life. Dalit girls should not be seen as passive members of society because they do in fact have agency.

Education can be a means to help girls overcome economic hardship, as it can potentially generate more economic opportunities. When it comes to caste and gender discrimination, the girls did not explicitly state if education helped them to overcome it. DSK's vocational schooling combined with social awareness-raising, however, is a key educational model that should be studied further. More research needs to be done to document if and how DSK's learning environment helps Dalit girls to overcome their discrimination.

In closing, there is no single remedy which will end the rampant discrimination that Dalit girls face. Dalit NGO leaders at Navsarjan do not believe that caste will end anytime in the near future. Dalit girls will continue to face social and educational exclusion, so their voices need to be fully heard in the Dalit Movement and Dalit families should be encouraged to value girls' education.

REFERENCES

Ambedkar, B.R. (1990). *Annihilation of Caste: An Undelivered Speech*. Edited by Anand, M.R. New Delhi: Arnold Publishers.

Annamalai, M. (Feb 2002). "Dalit Rights and Issues". In India Together. Retrieved online 12/1/07 from: http://www.indiatogether.org/dalit/articles/intro.htm.

Artis, E., Doobay, C., & Lyons, K. (January 2003). "Economic, Social, and Cultural Rights for Dalits in India: Case Study on Primary Education in Gujarat". New Jersey: Princeton University. Retrieved 11/29/07 online: http://www.wws.princeton.edu/research/PWReports/F02/wws591c_1.pdf.

Bandhu, P. (2005). "Dalit Women's Cry for Liberation: 'My Rights are Like the Sun, Will you Deny my Sunrise'?". In Rao, A. (Ed). (2005). *Issues in Contemporary Indian Feminism: Gender and Caste*. London: Zed Books.

Berreman, G. (1979). *Caste and Other Inequities: Essays on Inequality*. Meerut: Ved Prakash Vatuk, Folklore Institute.

Byapari, M. (2007). 'Is there Dalit Writing in Bangla?', in Economic and Political Weekly, October 13, 2007. p.4116-4120. http://www.epw.org.in/uploads/articles/11131.pdf

Carvalho, N. (2005). "Legalizing Child Marriages, an Attack Against Women, Says Churches and NGOs". AsiaNewsit.com online article from 10/8/2005. Retrieved online on 12/1/07 from: http://www.asianews.it/index.php?art=4303&l=en.

Chanana, K. (1993). "Accessing Higher Education – The Dilemma of Schooling: Women, Minorities, Scheduled Castes, and Scheduled Tribes in Contemporary India". In Altbach, P. & Chitnis, S. *Higher Education Reform in India: Experience and Perspectives*. New Delhi: Sage Publications.

Chitnis, S. & Altbach, P. (Eds). (1993). *Higher Education Reform in India: Experience and Perspectives*. New Delhi: Sage Publications.

Chopra, R. & Jeffery, P. (Eds). (2005). *Educational Regimes in Contemporary India*. New Delhi: Sage Publications.

Consortium for Research on Educational Access, Transitions, and Equity. "Access to Elementary Education in India: Country Analytical Review". R. Govinda, M. Bandyopadhyay. August 2007. Retrieved 11/10/07 online from: http://www.create-rpc.org/.

Council for Social Development (2006). *India Social Development Report*. New Delhi: Oxford University Press.

Dalit Foundation. http://www.dalitfoundation.org/

Department for International Development. http://www.dfid.gov.uk/

Dietrich, G. (2005). "Dalit Movement and Women's Movements". In Rao, A. (Ed). (2005*). Issues in Contemporary Indian Feminism: Gender and Caste.* London: Zed Books.

Dube, L. (2005). "Caste and Women". In Rao, A. (Ed). (2005*). Issues in Contemporary Indian Feminism: Gender and Caste.* London: Zed Books.

Freire, P. (1997). *Pedagogy of the Oppressed (2nd ed)*. New York: Continuum Publishing Company.

Government of India. (1950). "Constitution of India". Retrieved online 12/4/07 from: http://india.gov.in/govt/constitutions_india.php.

Government of India. (1989). "The Scheduled Castes and Scheduled Tribes (Prevention of Atrocities) Act, 1989". Retrieved online 11/30/07 from: http://india.gov.in/outerwin.htm?id/.

Government of India. (1991). Census of India, Volume II, p.419. New Delhi: Government of India.

Government of India. (1992-1997). "Eighth Five-Year Plan". Volume II, p.420. New Delhi: Planning Commission, Government of India.

Government of India. (1998). "National Policy on Education 1986 (as Modified in 1992)". New Delhi: Department of Education. Retrieved online 11/10/07 from: http://education.nic.in/policy/npe86-mod92.pdf.

Government of India. (2000-2001). "National Commission for SC/ST Report". New Delhi, India.

Government of India. (March 2002). "National Human Development Report". New Delhi: Planning Commission, Government of India.

Government of India. (2007). "National Report on 'A World Fit for Children'". Ministry of Women and Child Development. Retrieved online 12/12/07 from: http://www.unicef.org/worldfitforchildren/files/India_WFFC5_Report.pdf.

Govinda, R. & Diwan, R. (Eds). (2003). *Community Participation and Empowerment in Primary Education.* New Delhi: Sage Publications.

Gwatkin, D., Rutstein, S., Johnson, K., Pande, R.B., & Wagstaff, A. (2000). "Socio-Economic Differences in Health, Nutrition, and Population in India". HNP Population series, HNP/Poverty Thematic Group. Washington, DC: World Bank.

Hancock, D. & Algozzine, B. (2006). *Doing Case Study Research: A Practical Guide for Beginning Researchers.* New York: Teachers College Press.

Human Rights Watch. (Feb 2007). "Hidden Apartheid: Caste Discrimination Against India's 'Untouchables'". Retrieved 12/2/07 online: http://www.hrw.org/reports/2007/india0207/index.htm.

International Center for Research on Women (2005). "Too Young to Wed: Education and Action Toward Ending Child Marriage". Washington, DC: ICRW.

International Center for Research on Women (2006). "Son Preference and Daughter Neglect in India: What Happens to Living Girls?" Washington, DC: ICRW. Retrieved online 11/2/07 from: http://www.icrw.org/docs/2006_son-preference.pdf.

International Center for Research on Women (2007). "How to End Child Marriage: Action Strategies for Prevention and Protection". Washington, DC: ICRW.

Jain, T. (2005). "Caste: Don't Ask, Don't Tell". In India Together, 8/4/05. Retrieved online 11/15/07 from: http://www.indiatogether.org/2005/aug/.

Jain, P.C., Jain, S., & Bhatnagar, S. (Eds). (1997). *Scheduled Caste Women.* Jaipur, India: Rawat Publications.

Kapadia, K. (1995). *Siva and Her Sisters: Gender, Caste, and Class in Rural South India.* Boulder: Westview Press, Inc.

Kinsley, D. (1993). *Hinduism: A Cultural Perspective (2nd ed)*. Upper Saddle River, NJ: Prentice-Hall, Inc.

Kropac, M. (2007). *Dalit Empowerment and Vocational Education – An Impact Study*. New Delhi: Indian Institute of Dalit Studies.

Kumar, A. (Sep-Oct 2007). "Casteism in Higher Education". In Insight: Young Voices, Vol 1, no. 1. New Delhi: Insight Foundation.

Kumar, R. (Sep-Oct 2007). "Babasaheb Ambedkar on the Status of Indian Women". In Insight: Young Voices, Vol 1, no. 1. New Delhi: Insight Foundation.

Kumar, S. (February 26, 2006). "The Curse of Manual Scavenging". In India Together. Retrieved on 12/5/07 from: http://www.indiatogether.org/2005/feb/dlt-scavenger.htm.

Lewis, M. & Lockheed, M. (2006). *Inexcusable Absence: Why 60 Million Girls Still Aren't in School and What to do about it*. Washington, DC: Center for Global Development.

Louis, P. (2007). 'Lynchings in Bihar: Reassertion of Dominant Castes', in *Economic and Political Weekly*, Vol 42, no 44. Nov 3-9, 2007.

Manecksha, F. (April 2006). "Five Pledges for Dalit Shakti". In InfoChange Features. Retrieved on 12/9/07 from: http://www.infochangeindia.org/features349.jsp.

Mangalwadi, Vi. (2001). *The Quest for Freedom & Dignity: Caste, Conversion, and Cultural Revolution*. Willernia, MN: South Asian Resources.

Markandaya, K. (1954) *Nectar in a Sieve*. New York: Signet Classic, New American Library.

Maslak, M.A. (2003). *Daughters of the Tharu: Gender, Ethnicity, Religion, and the Education of Nepali Girls*. New York: Routledge Falmer.

Michael, S.M. (ed). (2007). *Dalits in Modern India: Vision and Values*. Second Edition. New Delhi: SAGE Publications.

Moon, M. & Pawar, U. (2005). "We Made History, Too: Women in the Early Untouchable Liberation Movement". In Rao, A. (Ed). (2005). *Issues in Contemporary Indian Feminism: Gender and Caste*. London: Zed Books.

Moon, V. (2001). *Growing up Untouchable in India: A Dalit Autobiography.* Lanham, Maryland; Rowman & Littlefield Publishers, Inc.

Nakumara, H. (Sep-Oct 2007). "State Level Conference of Dalit Women". In Insight: Young Voices. Vol 1, No 1. New Delhi: Insight Foundation.

Nambissan, G. (2003). "Social Exclusion, Children's Work, and Education: A View from the Margins". In Kabeer, N., Nambissan, G., & Subrahmanian, R. (Eds). *Child Labour and the Right to Education in South Asia: Needs versus Rights?* New Delhi: Sage Publications.

National Campaign on Dalit Human Rights (2002). *Dalits in the World of Globalization.* New Delhi: NCDHR.

National Commission for Scheduled Castes and Scheduled Tribes. (2001). "First Report: 2000-2001". Retrieved online 12/10/07 from: http://ncsc.nic/in.

National Commission for Scheduled Castes and Scheduled Tribes. (2002). "Educational Development of Scheduled Castes and Scheduled Tribes". Retrieved online 2/12/08 from: http://ncsc.nic.in/writereaddata/sublink2images/163.pdf.

National Commission for Scheduled Castes and Scheduled Tribes. (2004). "Second Report: 2003-2004". Retrieved online 12/10/07 from: http://ncsc.nic.in/index3.asp?ssid=226.

National Council of Churches of India. http://www.nccindia.in/

Navsarjan. http://www.navsarjan.org/home.asp

Rahman, M. (2006). "Indian Leader likens Caste System to Apartheid Regime". The Guardian. December 28, 2006. Retrieved online 11/19/07 from: http://www.guardian.co.uk/india/story/0,,1979157,00.html

Raj, E.S. (April 2001). *National Debate on Conversion.* Chennai, India: Bharat Jyoti.

Rajeshekar, VT. (June 1997). *Dalit: The Black Untouchables of India* (3rd ed). Gardena, CA: Clarity Press.

Rao, Anupama (Ed). (2005). *Issues in Contemporary Indian Feminism: Gender and Caste.* London: Zed Books.

Rawat, R. (Feb 2006). "The Problem". In Dalit Perspectives: A Symposium on the Changing Contours of Dalit Politics". Retrieved on 12/1/07 from: http://www.india-seminar.com/2006/558.htm.

Sabharwal, G. (2006). *Ethnicity and Class: Social Divisions in an Indian City.* New Delhi: Oxford University Press.

Seenarine, M. (1996). 'Dalit Women: Victims or Beneficiaries of Affirmative Action Policies in India: A Case Study'. From Columbia University talk, given on April 10, 1996. Retrieved online on 11/1/07 from: http://www.saxakali.com/Saxakali-Publications/dalit1.htm.

Seenarine, M. (2004). *Education and Empowerment among Dalit (Untouchable) Women in India: Voices from the Subaltern.* New York: Edwin Mellen Press.

Sen, Amartya (2000). 'Social Exclusion: Concept, Application, and Scrutiny', Working Paper, Social Development Paper No 1, Asian Development Bank, Bangkok, June. Retrieved online 2/2/08 from: http://www.adb.org/documents/books/social_exclusion/Social_exclusion.pdf

Shah, G., Mander, H., Thorat, S., Deshpande, S., & Baviskar, A. (2006). *Untouchability in Rural India.* New Delhi: SAGE Publications.

Shrirama (2007). "Untouchability and Stratification in Indian Civilization". In Michael, S.M. (ed). (2007). *Dalits in Modern India: Vision and Values.* Second Edition. New Delhi: SAGE Publications.

Stephen, C. (Sep-Oct 2007). "CEDAW and the Rights of Dalit Women". In Insight: Young Voices. Vol 1, No. 1. New Delhi: Insight Foundation.

Subramanian, M. (2006). *The Power of Women's Organizing: Gender, Caste, and Class in India.* Lanham, MD: Lexington Books.

Thorat, S. (2007). "Ambedkar's Interpretation of the Caste System, its Economic Consequences and Suggested Remedies". In Michael, S.M. (ed). (2007). *Dalits in Modern India: Vision and Values.* Second Edition. New Delhi: SAGE Publications.

UNAIDS. (2005). "Uniting the World Against AIDS: India (Country Report)". Retrieved online 12/12/07 from: http://www.unaids.org/en/Regions_Countries/Countries/india.asp.

UNESCO. www.unesco.org

UNESCO. (1985). "Towards Equality of Educational Opportunity: Inter-Country Exchange of Experiences". Bangkok: UNESCO Regional Office.

UNICEF. www.unicef.org

UNICEF. (2006). "HIV/AIDS in India". Retrieved online 12/12/07 from: http://www.unicef.org/india/hiv_aids_2587.htm.

United Nations. "UN Millennium Development Goals". http://www.un.org/millenniumgoals/

Webster, J. (2007). "Who is a Dalit?". In Michael, S.M. (ed). (2007). *Dalits in Modern India: Vision and Values*. Second Edition. New Delhi: SAGE Publications.

World Bank. (2007). *World Development Report 2007: Development and the Next Generation*. Washington, DC: The World Bank.

Zuniga, M. (2004). "The Feminization of AIDS". New York: International Women's Health Organization. Retrieved online 12/1/07 from: http://www.iwhc.org/resources/soroptimist041504.cfm.

CPSIA information can be obtained at www.ICGtesting.com
Printed in the USA
BVOW06s0159261114

376662BV00033B/422/P